DEATH NOTICES

DEATH NOTICES

Meg Hamill

Factory School
2007

Death Notices
by Meg Hamill

First Edition, Factory School 2007

Heretical Texts: Volume 3, Number 2
Series Editor: Bill Marsh

ISBN 1-60001-051-2

Cover art: Jess Perlitz
Production Assistant: Octavia Davis

Factory School is a learning and production collective engaged in action research, multiple-media arts, publishing, and community service.

factoryschool.org

So long as we see ourselves as essentially separate, competitive, and ego-identified beings, it is difficult to respect the validity of our social despair, deriving as it does from interconnectedness. Both our capacity to grieve for others and our power to cope with this grief spring from the great matrix of relationships in which we take our being. We are, as open systems, sustained by flows of energy and information that extend beyond the reach of conscious ego.

—Joanna Macy

It is October 15, 2006. We have been fighting in Iraq since March 19, 2003. This week researchers from the Johns Hopkins Bloomberg School of Public Health estimated that 600,000 Iraqi civilians have died since the beginning of the war, though they acknowledged a margin of error that ranged from 426,369 to 793,663 deaths. Since the start of this war, 2,759 American soldiers and 237 soldiers from 17 other countries, as well as 359 civilian contractors, have lost their lives in Iraq. 5,525 Iraqi police have reportedly lost their lives. I have no idea how many suicide bombers have exploded themselves into anonymous fireballs because some information, even in this age of information abundance, is still very difficult to find. I can't write that many obituaries, though I'm beginning to understand why I must. The fact that there are 367, 294 Iraqi civilians who we couldn't say are alive or dead right now is indicative of both the impossibility and the urgency of this project.

ta'ar, beloved— in pieces over there taken from this world by a missile that 15 cars burst into flames burning occupants to death cremating occupants alive while men and women tore frantically at the doors while wednesday morning in baghdad he was preceded in death by immediate occupants one and two and beloved relative three and onethousandandfour now his bicycle his scuffed shoes now his hopes and dreams his body in pieces over there ta'ar will be remembered as a one of many ones and as a blank as an incredibly loyal one as not one of the bad ones he connected with all ones especially living ones in a very special way no one may visit on thursday because his body is in pieces over there a service honoring the life will occur at nowhere you may send condolences to there

hammoud, malek— passed away peacefully while preparing lunch for some one the missile that killed him landed next to the westbound carriageway the missile that killed them this is all that is left of him now said a face holding out before him an oven pan dripping with blood survived by void and void and void and void and void and many voids and voids was he one of the good ones or one of the bad ones wondered far away some ones he will be sadly missed the missile that killed him now in pieces over there in lieu of flowers complicity the missile that killed them in lieu of flowers make donations in the form of whatever you do please make it urgent and springing from your heart in lieu of flowers please make it first you and the whole of you and then send it off right away to over there to where the ones are especially the ones left living *maybe when we undergo what we do something about who we are is revealed something that delineates the ties we have to others that shows us that these ties constitute what we are ties or bonds that compose us*

girl, young— was killed when two missiles whistled right through her many cotton layers to where the bones are standing on the central reservation trying to cross the road in a dense sandstorm an airplane a magnolia tree dropping its flowers in the rain i am riding my bicycle under it with a helmet on have been on a purifying diet am watching the rain come whistling right through her right to where the bones are mangled in a sandstorm we still have electricity send your active duty in the form of the truth is that the truth is actively living right here in your cell walls is heedless of boundaries the truth is dutifully our ribcage dense of the truth is a dense sandstorm where the bones are where the body may be viewed send flowers send the tree send flowers send the tree the truth is a sandstorm living here in lieu of complicity send flowers the tree a bicycle bones layers of cotton electricity

coles, sgt dominic r— IMMEDIATE RE-
LEASE december 28 2005 the depart-
ment of defense announced today the
death of a soldier who was supporting op-
eration iraqi freedom dominic r coles 25 of
jesup ga died in baghdad on dec. 26 when
his HMMWV came under attack during
combat operations by enemy forces using
small arms fire rocket-propelled grenades
and mortars dominic which portion
which expression of this pain to illumi-
nate as a more precise example of pain
dominic you signed up for killing and yet
you were killed you were guilty and yet
holding on to your rabbit ear were you
any more guilty than me dominic you
are here in this ink because i love you
because i have never met you because i
recognize your loved ones are swimming
through a slow moving body of pain right
now i recognize that collectively when
we wake up we wake up to the same slow
moving body of pain a slow moving body
of pain that no matter how hard i try i do
not really know that i might some day or
might never know

owner, electrical shop— was killed behind
his counter almost every day in baghdad
but this time two missiles in the sand-
storm every day in baghdad whistled
through a crowded market to a very
thick clouded marketplace this man is a
number he is a shop owner he is a num-
ber he is a shop owner he is a three days
ago in a sandstorm every day in baghdad
the numbers all around us the flame
shrouded cars all over baghdad flipped
upside down by the same missile the
only sure thing is this man is a number
is this man and this missile are expres-
sion machines this man and our missiles
expressing silence in their own explosive
or non-explosive way if you would like to
view the missile pay taxes on april 15 the
silence will be laid out bare in the bone
for us to wrap flowers around in lieu of a
funeral dirge silence in lieu of a proper
burial halliburton the only sure thing is
taxes is this man is a number this mis-
sile your check in the mail dropping
flowers from airplanes is taxes and dying
the only sure thing is this man and this
missile this silence splayed out within
and beneath them

i am driving with my sister and her husband in a four wheel drive car
    and we are kicking up dust
we are coming from band practice on the mesa
we are discussing the war in iraq
we are discussing tribal societies and beginning to argue
we are talking about jesus
we are talking about the president and his evil schemes
we are driving on bumpy dirt roads at ten miles per hour
at approximately 9:38 pm mountain standard time
we are talking about sunnis and shiites and there is a baby in the car
i am closing my eyes
i am closing my eyes and going to the center of me
it is dark in here but familiar
it is dark in here but i know where things are
here is my scapula here my floating rib here my heartbeat my uterus
here catalunya here pucallpa here the weminuche the shenendoa south
    van ness and 25th

it hurts to be tangled to these two
it hurts to be tangled in these words with these two and a baby in the car
we are talking about being married to each other
no we are talking about a bloodbath
no we are talking about the snowstorm in new england the day i was born
no we are talking about starting at the united nations and humbly
no we are talking about the farm where we were born and the geese that
    lived there with us
the heat is on full blast
the sky is so big
i am closing my eyes and feeling like the darkness in here isn't so dark as
    the darkness out there

sermed— as each survivor talked the dead
regained their identities as each identity
talked the dead regained their mourning in
baghdad as each morning in bagdhad cloud-
ed over in sand a slaughter on a syrian bus
as each syrian bus made its way through the
sand a bread beggar crossing the street
just like tuesday as each tuesday clouded
over with mourning a traffic jam outside
pleasanton as each traffic jam people tap
fingers on coffee on dread of the workday
on piles of bills of tax season of terror-
ists on higher degrees on civilian body
count 67% or 20,000 or 3/4 or more the
american pilot approached the crowded
market as the crowded market became
a thick cloud magnolias dropping from
an airplane 100% of the airplane dropped
magnolias there was a whistling after
the whistling there was blood sermed is
a name what else is sermed sermed is a
name that is hard to pronounce what else
is sermed is a hard to pronounce name
now a bag of bones and spilling blood in
a doorway what else is sermed 22% the
winds blow generally to the east which
leaves the western side clear most days
what else is sermed a symbol of how do
we live here in this country anymore and
what else is sermed is a mirror he is not
your reflection but look past him

koiri, lalan singh— a nepalese citizen who had traveled from nepal to earn money as a cook in the middle east was shot in the back of the head by the army of ansar al-sunna while lying face down in the dirt in late august 2004 in the photograph lalan you are wearing jeans with a white shirt tucked in to them and your arms are up above you in the dirt like you are about to dive into a swimming pool in the photograph there are twelve of you in a line all wearing white shirts with printed designs tucked into jeans neatly with your arms up above you in the dirt diving i see you chose your jeans carefully to fit the length of your legs lalan i can see how your jeans show off your body in a way that would have made certain people take note of certain parts of it i see your jeans have a leather label on the back right by the belt loops but i can't read what the label says i wonder if the label says levis or gap or lee or tommy hilfiger you don't have socks or shoes on lalan you are in a dirt pit that looks like a killing pit and i wonder if that killing pit was also a grave for you lalan most of your faces are nose down in the milky coffee colored dirt one man's head is turned to the side so that he looks like he is asleep but the rest of you have your noses in the dirt in an unnatural way with your arms above you so that it looks like you are playing a diving game and that you are about to dive into some slow moving body of water all together when the whistle blows as a team

you don't show people in agony on the

    air   you don't show

    a lot of dead bodies for taste

                  purposes

we take very seriously our responsibility

          to tell the story

as accurately and comprehensively

    as we can

        at the same time we're mindful

    of the sensibilities of our

        audience

who is steering us and where are we going
who could possibly stand up in front of all of us and say
i am in control of this ship and then explain to us where we are going
which stars we are navigating by and why
and if no one is steering then who do we blame
and if no one is to blame then take note of blame
take note before and after and beneath blame
illuminating blame
take note of the inherent fire of the deadness in blame

girl, 13 yr old— died when caught by a rico-
chet in the shoulder they were firing on
automatic agree with me everything up
to this point has been a postage stamp as
the wounded lay in the bazaar the british
soldiers drove away to see the edge of the
world peel down as if it were a postage
stamp the british then opened fire to be-
have like human beings it was 10:15 and
the market was very crowded most agree
that a local man started shooting with a
handgun human beings for good reason
the shooting lasted five minutes time-
less countryless heedless of boundaries
and then the edge of the world peeled
down as if it were a postage stamp there
were bullets going everywhere heedless
of boundaries of major hostilities agree
with me our eyes and ears are bunged
over 100 children's limbs in a month
agree with me our eyes and eyes are
bunged beautifully and without dissent
in lieu of dissent a work week a diaper a
beautiful river to fish in lieu of dissent
a magnolia tree dropping its flowers in
the rain

it is dark it is three am
the refrigerator belches
what was i dreaming about
i dreamed that i died and was looking down from above but death felt
    the same as being alive
i worried about whether i had died correctly because it felt like the
    same old thing
except i could watch my family imploding

i am 27
i live alone on a street one street east of a big street
today a suicide bomber blew up 32 people in iraq
today i rode my bike through the boarded upness of the city
i thought it's cold in this city it's primitive i feel transparent here
i thought the city is cracking open the city is not going to make it
i woke up twice to the tinkle of a bottle picker who came to pick
    through the recycling
i live in a yellow house with neighbors who smoke and own cats
who live quietly ten feet away from me on the other side of a thin
    100-year-old wall

qahtani, hadi bin mubarak— exploded himself into an anonymous fireball on april 11 2005 as part of a coordinated insurgent attack on a us marine base in the western iraq city of qaim the young saudi was said to have experienced a religious awakening after the world trade center attacks on the united states and soon thereafter dedicated himself wholly to allah clamoring to follow "those 19 heroes" of september 11 in lieu of flowers i am looking out the window of a small cafe and though there are lots of people on the street on bicycles walking by the window confidently in high heeled boots or sitting at tables drinking coffee there doesn't seem to be any religious awakening there doesn't seem to be any religious awakening whatsoever happening on this particular oakland street is it possible to wake up into different religious awakenings or is it the same religious awakening for all of us who are trying to wake up in that way and if it is the same then how come some embody this awakening by exploding themselves into anonymous fireballs and some do not is one awakening more true than another is one awakening more truly awake than another is one awakening in a fundamentalist sort of way more awake than someone not even trying to wake up sitting outside a cafe in a mediterranean climate taking the afternoon off work and drinking coffee confidently in high heeled boots

a study

by the project for excellence in journalism

of 40.5 hours of coverage

of the iraq war by

> *abc*
> *cbs*
> *nbc*
> *cnn and*
> *fox*

found that about half

> *the reports from*

> *embedded journalists*

showed combat action but not a single story

> *depicted people hit by*

> *weapons*

take note of blame take note the person i blame blames someone else
and so on
say blame until it loses its intrinsic blame
say it over and over again until blame is just a sound called blame
entirely unattached to blame

troops— WIPEOUT: GI'S KILL 300 IRAQI
TROOPS WITHOUT LOSING A MAN
(american abrams tank storming through
a cloud of dust the helmeted armor-clad
GI's driving it looking as invincible as the
tank itself) agree with me our eyes and
ears are bunged

piestewa, lori— the first american female
and native soldier killed in iraq was found
dead along with seven other bodies of us
soldiers in a hospital during the rescue of
american pow jessica lynch piestewa of
the hopi nation one of several indian na-
tions who declined us citizenship when it
was given to them in 1924 through the
indian citizenship act in favor of retain-
ing sovereign nationhood hopi who have
refused to acknowledge that the citi-
zenship act is in any way binding upon
them and continue to engage in such ex-
pressions of sovereignty as issuing their
own passports piestewa is survived by two
young children by her mother and father
in lieu of flowers jessica lynch who was a
long-time ally and confidante applied to
abc's extreme makeover home edition to
fulfill lori's dream of a home where her
entire family could live together and be
happy and so while the piestewa family
was sent off on a paid vacation to disney-
world ty pennington and his crew went
to work purchasing land and building a
home for them when a hopi is deceased
she comes back to the home mesas said
wayne taylor the tribal chairman as snow-
flakes coated his shoulders on a special
saturday afternoon the spirit returns to the
community and the family in the form of
moisture and this is lori coming back

among the hopi and maori there are people who do nothing but pray 24 hours a day 7 days a week 365 days a year every year of their lives that is all they do in rotation they pray around the clock for other people in this prayer is where they have seen some of the things that are about to happen the healing that is going to take place the advice that has been given to us is seek not to fight evil—do not fight it—let goodness take its place

beggar— passed away wednesday when missiles came screaming through the sand to destroy him when the missiles came screaming the bread beggar crossing the street with a dirt ring with beard with bone calloused feet with turban and WE LOVE YOU will keep you close to our hearts always close in the glove box tucked inside the insurance proof in the office parks big white gates close in the traffic outside where we work honking the missile through sand to destroy you mourning may happen in your cubicle in lieu of your cubicle mourning mourning may happen in your toyota in lieu of a traffic jam bodies not connected to their spirits anymore heaped in piles and bleeding mourning may happen WE LOVE YOU will keep you close to our hearts always will keep you screaming through sand to destroy you ALWAYS will keep our eyes appropriately bunged just like ALWAYS crossing the street just like tuesday will keep you in an office park just like always working through WE LOVE YOU to WE LOVE YOU working through WE LOVE YOU to not ironically but truly from the depths of us WE LOVE YOU

take note of love
say love over and over again until it loses its intrinsic love
until you realize love is completely unattached to love
until the inherent fire the inherent
deadness in love become clear
until love becomes not a feeling of love but a willingness
to extend oneself past oneself
past the inherent fire the inherent deadness in love

fatehah— passed away suddenly when our
muscles came swooping to the suburb of
diala bridge even as her mother was tend-
ing to one cow a donkey some chickens
fatehah joins the body count wherever
your religion is piling them in lieu of
pearly white gates the f/a-18 operation
iraqi freedom video game

now you can fly the most prolific carrier-based aircraft in the coalition arsenal load up with precision guided munitions and bring the forces of freedom to bear on the iraqi regime of terror

dagit, kevin— a 42-yr-old man from jefferson iowa who worked as a contractor for halliburton died in september 2005 while driving in a convoy of trucks that suddenly came under heavy fire representatives from halliburton came to the dagit house at midnight to report the death he was looking for adventure said his father he was doing what he wanted to do in lieu of flowers send the truth the truth is that the us army claimed the iraqi oil infrastructure contract was awarded to halliburton without competition because of a "national emergency" created by the pending war with iraq the truth is that cheney denied any relationship with halliburton as vice president the truth is that cheney received $205,298 in deferred salary from halliburton in 2001 $162,392 from the company in 2002 and $178,437 in 2003 the truth is i am using kevin dagit as an armored vehicle to complain about halliburton the truth is i am not here to complain about halliburton even though i'm glad i got to a little bit in lieu of flowers send this willingness to truly be alive inside of this clunky or graceful human form in lieu of flowers send a willingness to extend oneself past one's own clunky or graceful separate sense of self towards the larger expression of Self that is sometimes working as a waitress and sometimes praying for other people 24 hours a day   365 days a year and sometimes getting killed in iraq as a contractor for halliburton send it off right away to this slow moving body of pain expressed here as the passing as the absolute bodily rotting or burning of beloved kevin dagit in lieu of complaining a soul going up in lieu of complaining a soul freed from the construct of self going up and up

hamid, saman hassan— was hit by shrap-
nel while walking with her baby metal
balls and fragments designed to break up
on impact resulting in a huge increase
in surface area scattered into her brain
hemispheres her soft ligaments armpit
pupil patella breasts tender with milk and
being chewed ovaries intestines spleen
earlobe floating rib aorta flared nostril
kidney bones heartbeat muscle marrow
clavicle gluteus glandular blood type
unknown the heart a muscle the size
of a fist fatma six months old chubby
slightly charred found wriggling in
her arms change the information please
in lieu of flowers change it rapidly and
intersperse it with golf tournaments in
lieu of flowers our fists pumping inside
rib cages stuffed between the traffic re-
ports and kids in my country who are fat-
ter than ever this thursday said the front
page of a paper thrown onto the porch

marwa, tabarek and safa— died in the early morning dawn as we sheared through early morning rooftop sheep pens screwed into the belly of a cruise missile as we whistled through the side wall of a house splitting open as we are the rapture of dropping through the floor of a fighter jet as we snored slightly with three sisters in a split open room as we are one of the girls' legs hanging from a ceiling fan as we are molten magnesium chloride processed mainly from brines wells and seawater as we are dripping on the sisters resistant to dilute alkalies as we are the ammunition the frangible bullets the mother the father who were crazy about them whose love wasn't just ordinary love who are underneath the ceiling fan surrounded by pieces of you and me your neighbor my senator my country its alloys its metals its hands that were gathering and piecing together that are revolting and wringing together

klaharn, colonel mit— thailand army lieutenant age 43 from thailand assigned to 402nd engineering battalion died in karbala iraq on saturday december 27 2003 from hostile fire or from a car bomb attack or both thailand our ally whose population is 92.6% literate thailand our ally our confidante whose military inducts all 21-year-old males for two years of compulsory service thailand our bosom buddy our intimate our familiar thailand known as siam until 1939 thailand our amigo the only southeast asian country never to have been taken over by a european power our friend our partner thailand whose bloodless revolution in 1932 led to a constitutional monarchy thailand our cater-cousin our acquaintance our mate whose military expenditures average $1.775 billion annually as compared to our $370.7 billion annually in lieu of flowers i love you thailand in lieu of flowers from the bone of me thailand i love you

it is thanksgiving the war is here in this cafe wearing a baseball cap serving
    coffee listening to grateful dead bootlegs the war is pouring cream stirring
    in sugar
the sun came up again over the war urging it on saying
be delgado be muscular look up quiet down and listen
when they break ground for skyscrapers in san francisco they find the
    carcasses of boats they find the bones of gigantic camels embryonic in
    the mud
the tusks the mahogany the sun trapped in a fish bone trod on by us
with varying degrees of consciousness through every splicing of human gene
through every pedicure through every airplane circling
thank you president for showing up in my void this morning beating with
    my own heartbeat thank you for this latte thank you
for attaching me to the belly of a cruise missile and what this teaches me
    about my own essence and getting past shame to feeling the crisis that is
    me there dropping through the floor of a fighter jet towards some market-
    place crowded with people buying bread
thank you for the center of me where it is dark and comforting and i know
    my way to the soft parts of my body the ones that are harboring too much
    impatience still too much fat
thank you for big bags spilling of wheat
thank you that our turkey is organic and free-range
thank you to all the people camped out in crawford texas today thank you
to all the people who are dying today and where are you now that you are
    dead are you fluttering emotionally hovering a few feet from the floor not
    far from here
remind me how anything could be just gone ever remind me where you
    think it would go if not to sit beside you while the war is on and your
    coffee getting cold

somewhere near a thousand shiite pilgrims—
were trampled to death crushed against
barricades drowned in the tigris thirty
feet below wednesday when a procession
across a baghdad bridge was engulfed in
panic over rumors that a suicide bomber
was at large family and friends are invited
to wander about lifting sheets in search
of their kin and upon finding them to
shriek out loud in grief and pound their
chests with their fists or else to collapse
on the earth nearby family and friends
are invited to become bare-chested and
jump into the tigris to recover the bodies
that are floating downstream families
and friends are invited to form in large
packs on the beaches as bodies float
down river as children flounder in the
muddy waters trying to reach dry land
family and friends are invited to visit
the two-lane 300-yard-long bridge that
is littered in sandals lost in the pushing
and panic family and friends are urged
to pay homage to the barriers meant to
keep sunni and shiite extremists out of
each other's neighborhoods at either end
of the bridge

mousa, baha— was killed from repeated beatings by soldiers of the queen's lancashire regiment in a room at darul dhyafa where he allegedly received more beatings than the other hotel workers arrested at the same time i could hear him moaning through the walls after the beatings saying that he was bleeding from his nose and that he was dying i heard him say i am dying blood blood i heard nothing from him after that read the witness statement of mr al-mutari a fellow hotel worker who was arrested at the same time and also beaten by the british soldiers at darul dhyafa said his father in a witness statement before the high court he had a badly broken nose the skin on one side of his face had been torn away to reveal the flesh beneath the skin on his wrists had been torn off and the skin on his forehead torn away and there was no skin under his eyes either i literally could not bear to look at him

another hood on top of the first hood

water was given to us by pouring it through the hood so that
we had to lick the droplets through the hood

freezing water was poured on us and this was very painful as the temperatures in detention were 40 degrees plus

we were prevented from sleeping for three days

soldiers would mention some english names of stars of foot-ball players and request us to remember them or we would be beaten severely

the soldiers would surround us and compete as to who could kickbox one of us the furthest to make us crash into a wall

acklin, sgt michael d II— battery c 1st
battalion 320th field artillery regiment
101st airborne division (air assault) from
louisville kentucky was killed when two
101st airborne division UH-60 black hawk
helicopters collided in mid-air over mosul
iraq on november 15 2003 and now your
face that signed up for killing is everywhere
now i type your name into my ibook g4
and find the details of you neatly orga-
nized in t-charts with photographs along-
side all the other mortified-looking faces
of those who were killed who signed up
for killing but where is the t-chart for
those who signed up for nothing and yet
got killing instead where is the t-chart for
the mothers who are beating their chests
in the shrapnel-scarred scenes in our rib-
cage the truth is there is a discrepancy
in available information the truth is this
discrepancy is worth getting all riled up
about because it points towards our com-
plete inability to take on the suffering of
the world that is happening and seems to
be happening continually with our tax
dollars with our resources in our name
the truth is this discrepancy is devoid of
significance is peanuts is tunnel vision
in the face of helicopters colliding in the
face of families imploding and vital forces
that aren't ripe yet and not that forceful
yet being forced out of their bodies and
not knowing where to go or who to haunt
or what to do in lieu of flowers examine
your we in lieu of flowers examine how
this discrepancy in available information
is worth raising your fist about and at the
same time how it is purposeless how it
is good for nothing examine how the ex-
amination of it is just as prone to egoic
fundamentalism as the non-examination
donations may be sent in the form of the
truth which will without fail steal every
point of view that we try to fixate upon
it

26 civilians mostly children gathering candy from us troops— i record here with pro-
found sorrow with my heart in a void the
size of a fist and pumping these children
out through the void that is my heart
muscle who were fascinated by helmet
and flak-jacket clad american soldiers in
armored vehicles these who were voids
on bicycles whirling around in ribcages
beating whose bones were growing even
as we armored through their neighbor-
hood in loud in incredibly loud vehicles
who were pleading with the 18-year-olds
from my mississippi river my kalama-
zoo my arkansas ozarks and fields saying
please saying please for hersheys bars and
caramellos who were killed by shrapnel
and the voids in our ribcages where the
muscle the size of a fist should be when
a suicide bomber in an explosives-laden
suv drove into a lower-middle class resi-
dential district of baghdad populated
mainly by shiites and detonated himself
and detonated his vehicle into the void
where the heart should be a boy said my
cousin was killed this is part of his bi-
cycle this is part of his ribcage that held
a heart now hold it in our void in our
women draped in black near the shrapnel-
scarred scene in our ribcage

if anyone gets too close to us we fucking

           waste them

it's kind of a shame because

it means we've killed a lot of innocent

                     people

                it gets to the point where

        you can't wait to see guys with

                  guns

        so you start shooting everybody

has the universe come to itself through you and i as an intricate mode of
   conscious reflection
has it come through bruce springsteen rush limbaugh jamaica kincaid dick
   cheney
as an intricate mode of self-conscious reflection
has it come through all the people in the airport on cellphones saying we're
   at the gate now
we're at the gate now we're at the gate
now
do we and this war and the big cranes along the oakland port and tuck and
   patti and christmas coming all
originate and then reflect ourselves back to the universe in the very curvature
   of space

imagine the earth before there were any beings with eyes or brains on it
did it have a way of looking at itself back then

al-shamari, qais hashem— the secretary
of iraq's council of judges was shot dead
at the age of three score and two together
with his son in an ambush by armed men
in a car the judge and his son had just left
home and were driving in eastern baghdad
in lieu of flowers examine your we exam-
ine who lost who or if who was lost at all
examine how to lose who without having
who in the first place examine what va-
cancy can be made for the vacancy that
already exists in we

20 people in procession— died on the first
day of may in 2005 when a suicide bomber
drove his car into a funeral procession for
talab wahab a senior KDP official who had
been assassinated by armed men a few days
earlier in the town of tal afar near mosul

in lieu of flowers i am learning of
the vulnerability of a great blue heron
perched at the rim of a slough near the
san francisco bay just northeast of the
golden gate bridge who is four feet tall
with a wingspan of six feet who weighs
only eight pounds and lays light green
eggs and stands atop a drainage pipe peer-
ing into the mercury-laden mud fishing
for crabs

of how our skins our jackets our feathers
our hairs tangling into matted knots on our
heads become levees so that we don't spill
out ourselves in rushing brief floods and be-
come each other   wholly

indiscriminately

twin suicide bombers— were killed sunday when they strapped explosives to themselves and suspiciously wandered into iraq's interior ministry where ministers and the us ambassador were attending a parade to mark police day police shot one of the bombers because he looked suspicious but the bullets detonated the explosives strapped to his body as police crowded around the remains the second suicide bomber blew himself up wreaking carnage killing 28 people and seriously wounding 25 both bombers were dressed in iraqi police uniforms

i am thinking all of a sudden of how we come into the world attached to mothers by slippery blue cords of how from the onset we are given over to the other vulnerably and without the capacity for dissent i am thinking of the very rudimentary sense of self that exists at that moment of being at the other end of a blue and slippery cord a sense of self that barely discriminates between itself and the bigger body that it came from

if you really want to effect change become heretical law-abiding
scientific spiritual lonely crowded
become a hopi person who does nothing but pray for other people 24
hours a day 365 days a year
every year of their lives
become a suicide bomber become an oil baron become a us soldier
from cerulean kentucky
who is 21 years old stationed somewhere outside fallujah
become an iraqi person who died from a paveway laser-guided bomb
built for the us navy by the raytheon corporation at 870 winter
street in waltam massachusetts
if you really want to effect change become a person who died from
being 95 become
a person buried at wounded knee become
a dead person who goes through the tunnel of light and finds someone
inarticulatably important to them waiting at the other side of the
tunnel
and then for some reason
comes back to life
become a person who fishes become a person who goes to wall street
to make money
become a person who goes to wall street to be moved to tears become
people who
cut logs become rainforest people become island people
if you really want to effect change become an expatriate become a
muslim a christian a buddha
become enlightened become the articulation of your own numinous
extraordinary self
become a person who composts a person who has worms
become in love become disgusted with the world become someone
who has lost their courage
become someone who has lost their hope become someone who has
awakened
from losing their hope
who has awakened to what is beneath even that
beneath even losing all hope

12 iraqi army recruits— loving brothers of space space and space beloved husbands of space were killed on february second by armed men on a road near kirkuk loving fathers of space and space and space according to reports the armed men stopped a convoy of iraqi army recruits in the village of zab near kirkuk forced them to lie facedown on the dirt road and shot them one by one devoted grandfathers devoted fathers-in-law of space

at least 68 people— were killed in suicide car bomb attacks in southern iraq what is real is that these people remain neither alive nor dead to us here but nameless in this light breeze from the northeast at 3 mph with humidity at 82%

udishu, janet and sadaa— were killed
when gunmen in basra blocked their taxi
with a car ran out in front and fired point
blank at the women the women were
sisters the women were christians the
women worked for a us firm that offered
top-notch infrastructure development con-
tracting the lucrative projects to us corpo-
rations thus the women were traitors the
women were infidels the women were
paying their own bills the women were
shot at point blank in a taxi outside their
home near an assyrian church in central
basra the women were not yet forty the
women were a blip in our radar the wom-
en were beautiful the women were just
a little above average the women were
holy women the women were copying
the version of women they learned from
their women the women were anatomi-
cally women the women were oppressed
the women were free the women fell
outside our relationship to women and
thus weren't really women the women
were mothers the women were children
of women

even though we're making a mess of things
we are still hurtling together
through space
rotating anywhere from 700 to 1,038 miles per hour depending on
where on the earth's surface we happen to be standing

what does it mean to lose courage
if we are hurtling through space like this anyway
where would the courage go if it was lost

fatima's uncle and his wife— died when us bullets shattered their knees shattered their home killed all of their chickens deliberately one by one with heartfelt sadness i am beginning to understand how it is that my subjectivity is an important piece of your subjectivity an important piece of the mangled bodies that are piling in ditches near the overpass where we are struggling collectively with deception and hot coffee cups and internet dating *there's a picture of the world trade center*

    hanging up by my bed

    and i keep one in my flak jacket

every time i feel sorry for these people i look
at that i think

    they hit us at home

    and now it's our turn

    i don't want to say payback but it's
pretty much

    payback

a headless iraqi corpse lying in a street one arm draped in protection around a dead child who is lying on the corpse— with profound sadness we cannot come together each other in america without finding a mangled body claiming what is silent between us anymore we cannot meet for coffee without a heap of bodies waiting by the side of a road waiting in the gaps in conversation between us anymore we cannot enjoy a moment of affection of touching of a hand resting in the shallow in between your breasts without also coming to rest in a shallow ditch where blood is congealing on a head that is not attached to a body and a baby on the body not attached to a spirit anymore in lieu of flowers do not kick the bodies underneath the table that are gathering between us without noticing without taking note of their limpness their inability to hold onto each other their inability to pray or to breathe

hassoun, zaidoun fadel— beloved twelfth grader nearing his high school graduation beloved nearing a third cycle of newly generated cells beloved nearing new automobiles new appliances new levis beloved reaching for new depths of struggle for exerting one's utmost beloved reaching for the true meaning of jihad nearing new the beloved of one's life drowned after being thrown into the river tigris by a us army patrol in samarra in january 2004 when our beloved sergeant perkins ordered the men thrown into the river because he didn't want them to think we were soft or weak didn't want them to see our beloved separateness becoming confused our separateness becoming stitched so unbreachably together didn't want them to see the fissures beginning to show beginning to destabilize the very nucleus of our dominant paradigm zaidoun died calling out the name of his cousin marwan marwan screaming help me marwan help me

fifteen members of the al-khafaji family—
died while fleeing the fighting in haidariya
on march 31 2003 their pickup was de-
stroyed by a missile from an apache heli-
copter they are survived by razek al-kazem
al-khafaji who lost all six of his children
his wife his mother his father three broth-
ers and three sisters-in-law his network
his thread his porous self letting other
selves into his self his void his selfhood his
opening into others his opening into void

today saddam hussein said i am not afraid of execution
execution is cheaper than the shoe of an iraqi
and i spent a long time eating a blueberry muffin trying to figure out
    what he meant by that
today i went on a tour of the east bay sewage treatment plant
where the intricate art of microbes was occurring as
seagulls dropped used tampons on the concrete by our feet
today i saw a bat ray from the underneath saw its lips sucking in air
and felt its cartilage skin which was so much smoother than mine
today there are record low temperatures in denver and in the pictures
    people are uncomfortably crossing streets in very heavy coats
today in bolivia there is a group of indigenous women living in an
    andean ecovillage toiling over wool hammocks and socks
today in california stanley tookie williams is awaiting execution and
    people are rallying around his cause
today the wetlands in the san francisco bay are sucking up nitrates that
    have spilled into the bay from the central valley and are exuding them
    into the air as a non-toxic gas
today the un climate talks are entering a key phase
today in egypt three are dead in poll clashes
and microsoft invests 1.7 billion in india
today i am not working and am sitting instead in a cafe listening to
    lifescapes inner peace
today i mailed a christmas card to an old lover in spain and to a film-
    maker in new york city
who used to share a house with me when i was 21 years old
today the people dying in iraq feel very far away and so do the bullets
    that are killing them
today physicists everywhere are realizing that the universe articulates
    itself wholly and
uniquely in each living and non-living thing
that it never shows up only partway just like we don't show up only
    partway to each other
or do we
today inside of me it feels like i am showing up only partway to myself
today california bank and trust is taking money in and letting money go
today adom hair braiding doesn't have any customers yet
today i'll go food shopping and try to remember the interior articulation
    of reality within myself
as i am sampling cheese and choosing what kind of butter and scooping
    rice into a plastic bag

**about 20 civilians in an apartment build-
ing on abu taleb street in baghdad**— died
when two missiles from a us aircraft hit
the building and a nearby row of shops in
the poor baghdad neighborhood of as-shaab
in lieu of flowers the articulation of your
own numinous immediate self

al-jamadi, manadel— died from pressure to the chest and extreme difficulty breathing during a cia interrogation in the prisoner's shower room at abu ghraib on november fourth 2003 he was suspended by his wrists which had been handcuffed behind his back in an impossible way as the guards released the shackles and lowered al-jamadi to the floor blood gushed from his mouth as if a faucet had been turned on in the photograph of his corpse the us soldiers are grinning family and friends are invited to remain calm after the images are released family and friends are asked not to become religious fanatics or go bombing through crowded marketplaces once the photos are released family and friends are asked to politely ignore the mad feeling that follows the images of the us soldiers grinning next to the torchered man being released family and friends with a spike going through you searching for meaning in the spike going through this too will pass says the void family and friends are invited to day to day living to breathing in deeply after the images of the torchered man being released

things on this planet seem to be getting really bad probably
worse than we could imagine
even those of us who are trying to imagine those who
see some benefit in imagining
who stay up late reading articles and books about the destruction of
everything trying to get the grey matter in our brains to be able to imagine
probably aren't even imagining the half of it

the bad things have to do with numbers and statistics that say
most of this precious beautiful thing is gone from the planet forever and
    most of this other thing has been all chopped down
and the rate of this weird disease that makes relating
to other people impossible has gone up this shocking percent
and the ice caps everywhere are receding this much each year
and there are this many countries being occupied and this many bombs
    being made each day and this many languages obliterated
and the ratio of ceo to worker salary in america is this huge number in the
    hundreds
that keeps getting bigger each year
to one
and so on
this data is everywhere about everything all the time

is awareness of these bad things that are too statistical and numerical and
    everything
everywhere to list here
and of the stunning things too
of the stunning moments like yesterday near the farallon islands when a
    50-foot humpback whale nudged each diver gently in turn after they un-
    tangled her from a mess of nylon crab lines

in itself curative

could it be that healing begins at the moment when
we learn to sustain our gaze
on all the bad and all the stunning things just
keep our eyes looking
past the time when we want to stop looking

ten members of the subhi family— died
when cars from the garage were hurled
violently into the walls of their house in
nasiriyah on march 23 2003 when debris
from the bombs falling was flung for 300
yards in all directions and didn't spare
them or their young people or their dinner
that was cooking didn't spare their hopes
their skin ailments their unpaid bills
didn't spare their cells functioning health-
ily or their interconnectedness their belief
their disbelief in american values didn't
spare the dishes the rugs or the ones who
didn't die the father the 18-yr-old daughter
in the hospital still a year later waiting to
hear whether doctors will or will not am-
putate her right leg

i want to create a bridge between all the different kinds of humans
all the dead ones even all
the oppressed and all the caged ones
all the 18-year-old ones who signed up for killing

all the ones who live in deserts the ones with a railroad going through them
flying prayer flags

could we define grace as being acted through

i don't know how to make bridges
i don't know how to be acted through

and yet organic systems seem to organize themselves
burrowing owls some vetch taking root
snowy egrets
new zealand sea slugs
hermaphroditic worms heirloom tomatoes our
kidneys our optical nerves
don't seem to have any burning questions about the difficulties inherent in
functioning
don't seem to feel the need to say i like you
but do not really like you or you

hamdani, ali (20), hussein (18), and mohamed (9)— died when one ea-6b prowler jet fired either one HARM anti-radar missile or one paveway laser-guided bomb built for the us navy by the raytheon corporation at 870 winter street in waltam massachusetts upon one crowded marketplace in the poor shi'a neighborhood of shuala where the brothers lived in the same house with one mother who in lieu of flowers was pounding her chest amid the shrapnel-scarred scene in the street in lieu of flowers my three boys are dead in lieu of flowers what is left for me to live for my whole life has been destroyed i nursed them all my life in lieu of flowers and now they're gone

10 iraqi troops— were killed friday when guerrillas armed with machine guns and rocket propelled grenades stormed an iraqi army post in baghdad just as defense secretary donald rumsfeld in his pre-christmas visit to a marine base in the subdued rebel stronghold of fallujah was telling us combat troops that their numbers would fall as iraqi forces were trained to take over ten iraqi troops with a spike going through you ten iraqi troops with a reuters news story written up immediately about you you who it is most difficult to devote poems to you without faces who are teetering on the edge of innocent you faceless teetering on the edge of what i am able to relate to ten soldiers with a guerrilla going through you you whose bodies were filled with livers and spleens whose bodily organs were exact replicas of my bodily organs whose olfactory nerves worked just like my olfactory nerve ten troops with a slow moving body of water with a gentle wind blowing through you the bone of the world feels breathy and full of wind and startlingly wierd

the kingdom of heaven is right here said jesus

using his bone of the world to deliver the message to the bones of the world

once one bone understands the message

it is like bones knitting together again after being broken in an accident

there is that coming together again ability within all the bones

hatab, nagem sadoon— died at a makeshift holding center near nasiriya in june 2004 from suffocation caused by a broken bone in the throat after being repeatedly beaten and repeatedly kicked by us marine guards and left lying in pride and ego left lying naked in futility in the baking sun for several hours in lieu of flowers return to this way of being called blame return to this way of being called beneath blame where there is a silence we get glimpses of sometimes a ringing silent space that doesn't go anywhere that is hiding from itself that like sunlight indiscriminately enters into every place that has this flaming red expression of itself called blame

madlul, amir— died in a us bombing raid on april 8 2003 when his home was destroyed when his body was carbonized when he was recognized by a brother only by his car keys which had been seared into his body flesh from the heat of the blast no services are scheduled no apologies no images on american television are scheduled no paradigm shifts no pullouts no protests by the american people are scheduled

hamoodi, zainab— died on april 5 2003 while waiting out an attack with 13 other members of her family in her family's air raid shelter when the adjoining house was struck by two missiles and collapsed into the shelter burying the entire family in rubble and killing ten of them interment to reoccur in our heart voids interment to reoccur in our tangled web in our ribcages interment to reoccur when south korea pulls one third of their troops out of iraq interment to reoccur in the cell walls of our esophagi interment to reoccur in our six billion solitudes which are so very different than six billion isolations interment to reoccur in our penetrating questions in our yearning that comes from deep within the sleepwalking and yet is something already awake within the sleeping pointing out yearning out towards the non-sleepwalking because there is no other way

This book is full of information that was found. Credit is due to the following people, websites, and sources for providing specific phrases, sentences, paragraphs, and factual information for this project; however credit is also due to countless domestic and foreign news sites online where I found names of people and places and events. There were so many sites that I did not in any way keep track. I list here, in no particular order, those whose words I borrowed more directly and the news sites that I visited regularly: Joanna Macy from World as Lover, World as Self and Despair, and Personal Power in the Nuclear Age, icasualties.org, iraqbodycount.org, Lester Crystal, executive producer for The News Hour with Jim Lehrer, www.bbc.co.uk, CNN spokesman Matthew Furman, Judith Butler from Precarious Life, nytimes.com, Larry Merculieff from an address to the Aleut Elders in Alaska, the witness statement of Kifah Taha Al-Mutari, statements from an anonymous Lieutenant, Ramadi, Iraq, and an anonymous U.S. Army Corporal, both quoted in The London Evening Standard.